W9-AOU-131

CHINA
FOR YOUNGER READERS

Edited by Ye Yonglie and Wei Wen
Illustrated by Jia Yanliang

DOLPHIN BOOKS BEIJING

First Edition 1989

Hard Cover: ISBN 0-8351-2212-3 ISBN 7-80051-270-3
Paperback: ISBN 0-8351-2213-1 ISBN 7-80051-271-1

Published by Dolphin Books
24 Baiwanzhuang Road, Beijing, China

Distributed by China International Book Trading Corporation
(Guoji Shudian), P.O. Box 399, Beijing, China

Printed in the People's Republic of China

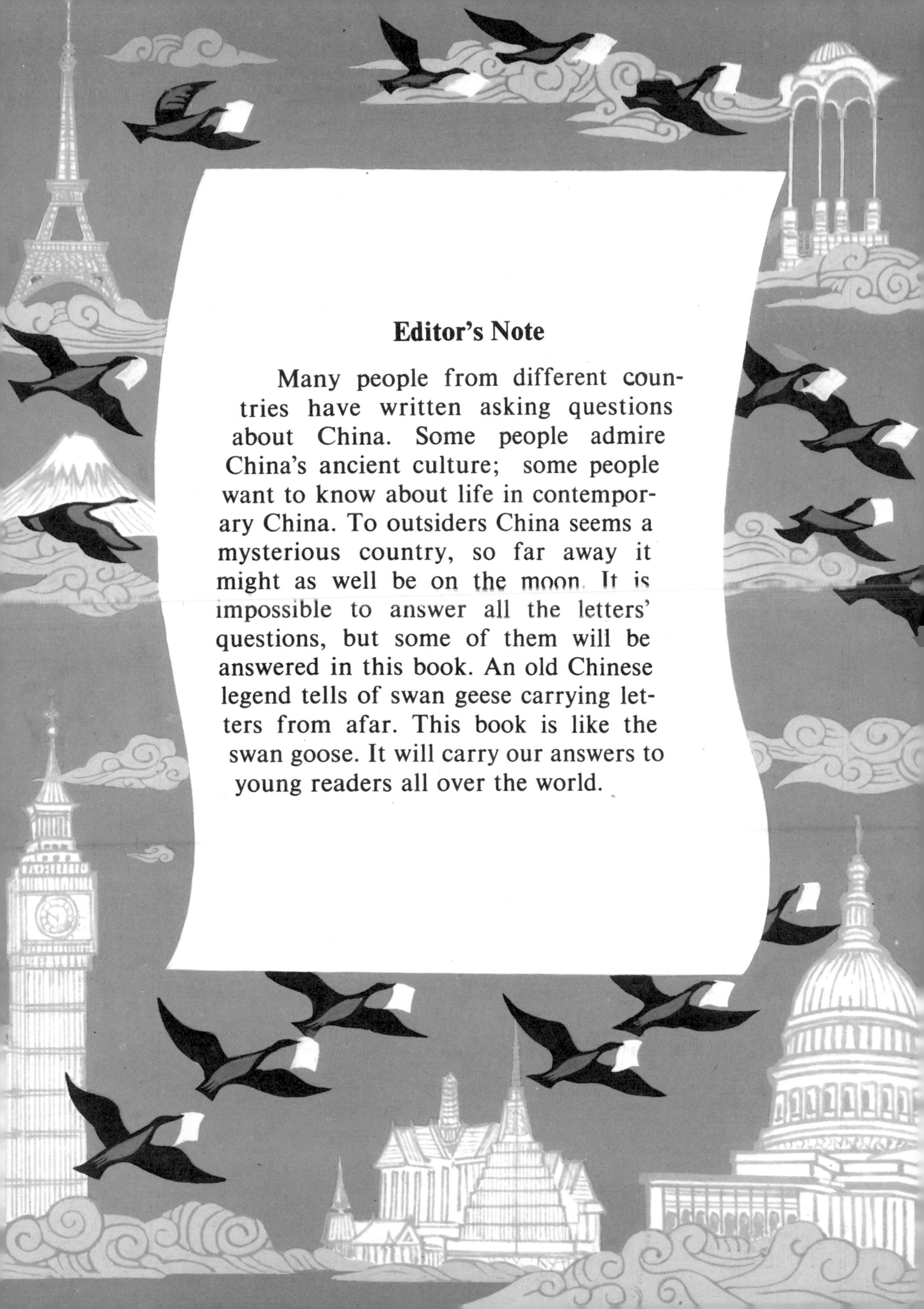

Editor's Note

Many people from different countries have written asking questions about China. Some people admire China's ancient culture; some people want to know about life in contemporary China. To outsiders China seems a mysterious country, so far away it might as well be on the moon. It is impossible to answer all the letters' questions, but some of them will be answered in this book. An old Chinese legend tells of swan geese carrying letters from afar. This book is like the swan goose. It will carry our answers to young readers all over the world.

Contents

Chinaware and China	1
China's Geographic Location	5
A Mountainous Country	7
A Complex Topography	10
The Yellow River and the Yangtze River	11
A Varied Climate	13
Administrative Divisions	15
Metasequoia, a Living Fossil	18
The Giant Panda	19
Solving the Problem of Feeding the Population	21
Developing Industry	23
A Multinational Country	25

The Chinese Language 28
Learning Chinese 30
Distinctive Art 31
Beijing Opera
—A Comprehensive Performing Art 33
Who Was Confucius? 36
Ancient Poems 37
The Great Wall 39
Four Great Inventions 41
Traditional Chinese Medicine 49
Chinese Cuisine 51
Decline of Feudal China 54
The Founding of New China 55
Beijing—An Ancient and A New City 57

Chinaware and China

Exquisite ancient China's chinaware is exhibited in the museums of many countries. Why is it called china? Most likely because Westerners liked the porcelain that came from China

so much that they named it for the country it came from. The name china comes from the Sanskrit, meaning "land of Qin." In China's history Qin was the first powerful feudal dynasty (221-207 B.C.) that had unified the country. Qin Shi Huang, the first emperor of the Qin Dynasty, is famous for building

China's Great Wall. China's own name for itself is *Zhongguo*, which means "the central state." Three thousand years ago the central part of the country, surrounded by many vassal states, was directly under the rule of the king, and it was called the central state (*zhongguo*). Gradually the whole country was named *Zhongguo*.

China's Geographic Location

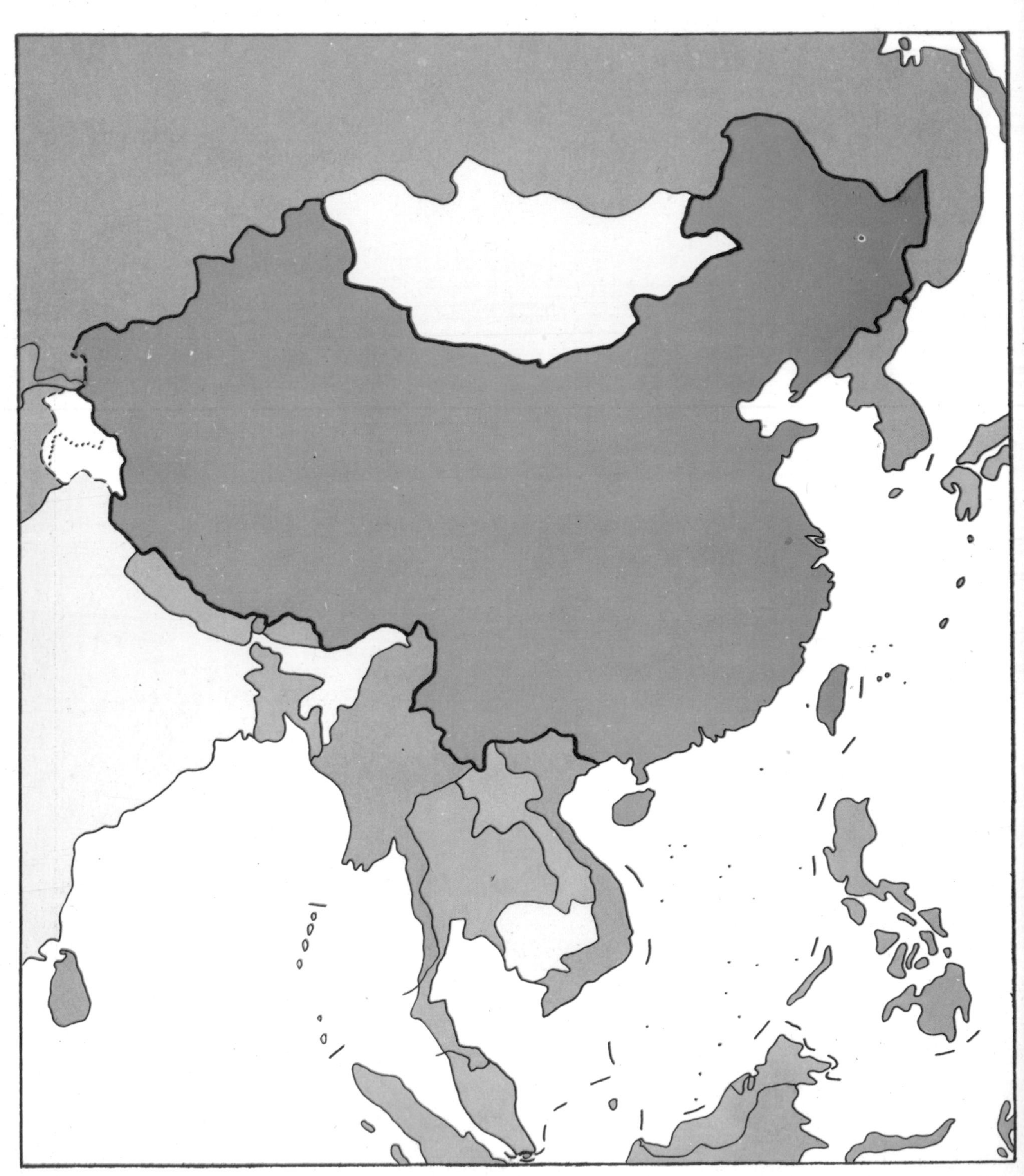

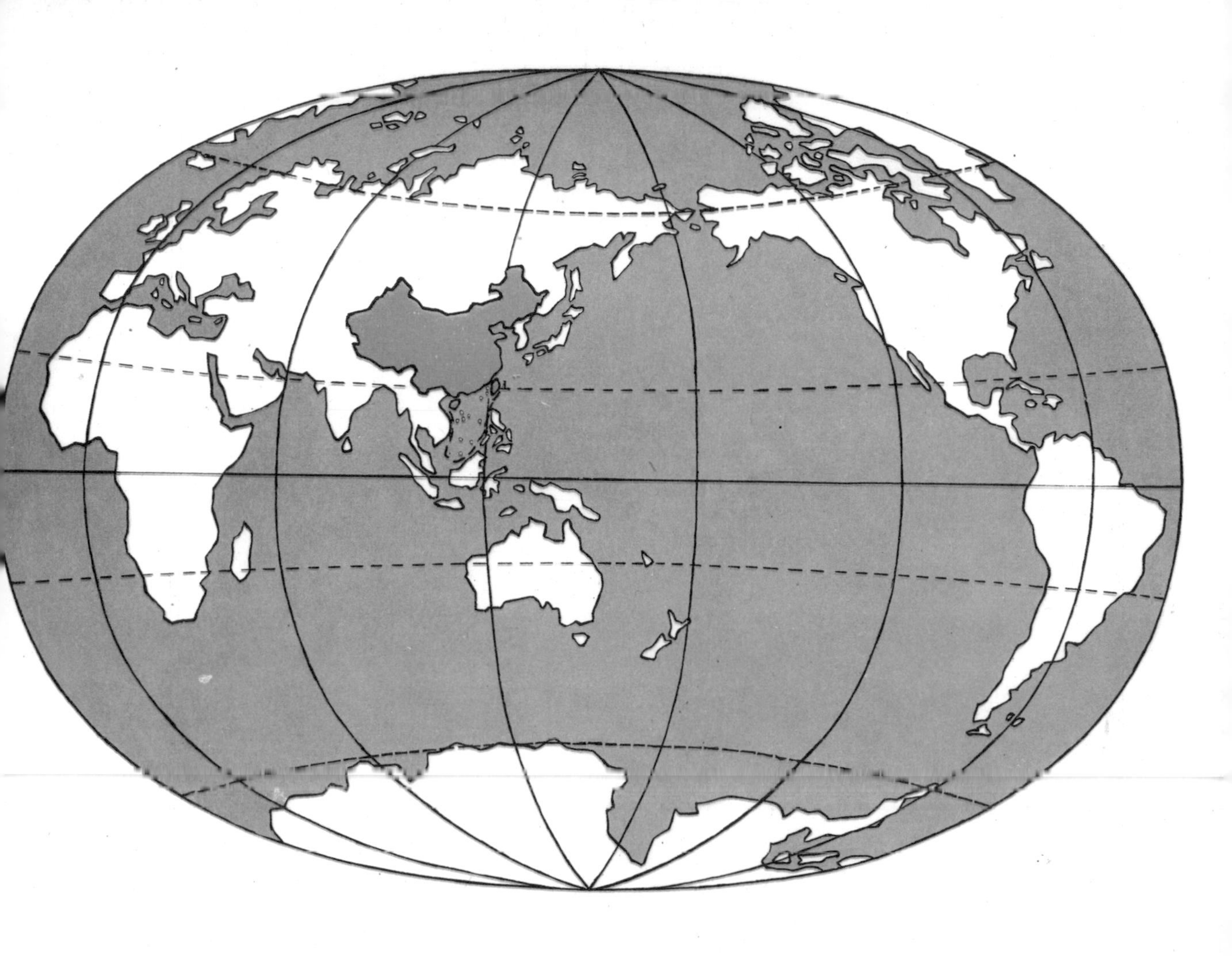

China is situated in the eastern part of Asia. A map of China looks like a rooster standing on the west coast of the Pacific Ocean.

China's land area covers approximately 9.6 million square kilometres, almost as big as Europe, making China, after the Soviet Union and Canada, the third largest country in the world.

China is bordered by Korea in the east; the Soviet Union in the northwest and northeast; the People's Republic of Mongolia in the north; Afghanistan and Pakistan in the west; India, Nepal, Bhutan, and Sikkim in the southwest; Burma, Laos and Viet Nam in the south. Across the East China Sea to the east and the South China Sea to the southeast it faces Japan, the Philippines, Malaysia, Brunei and Indonesia.

A Mountainous Country

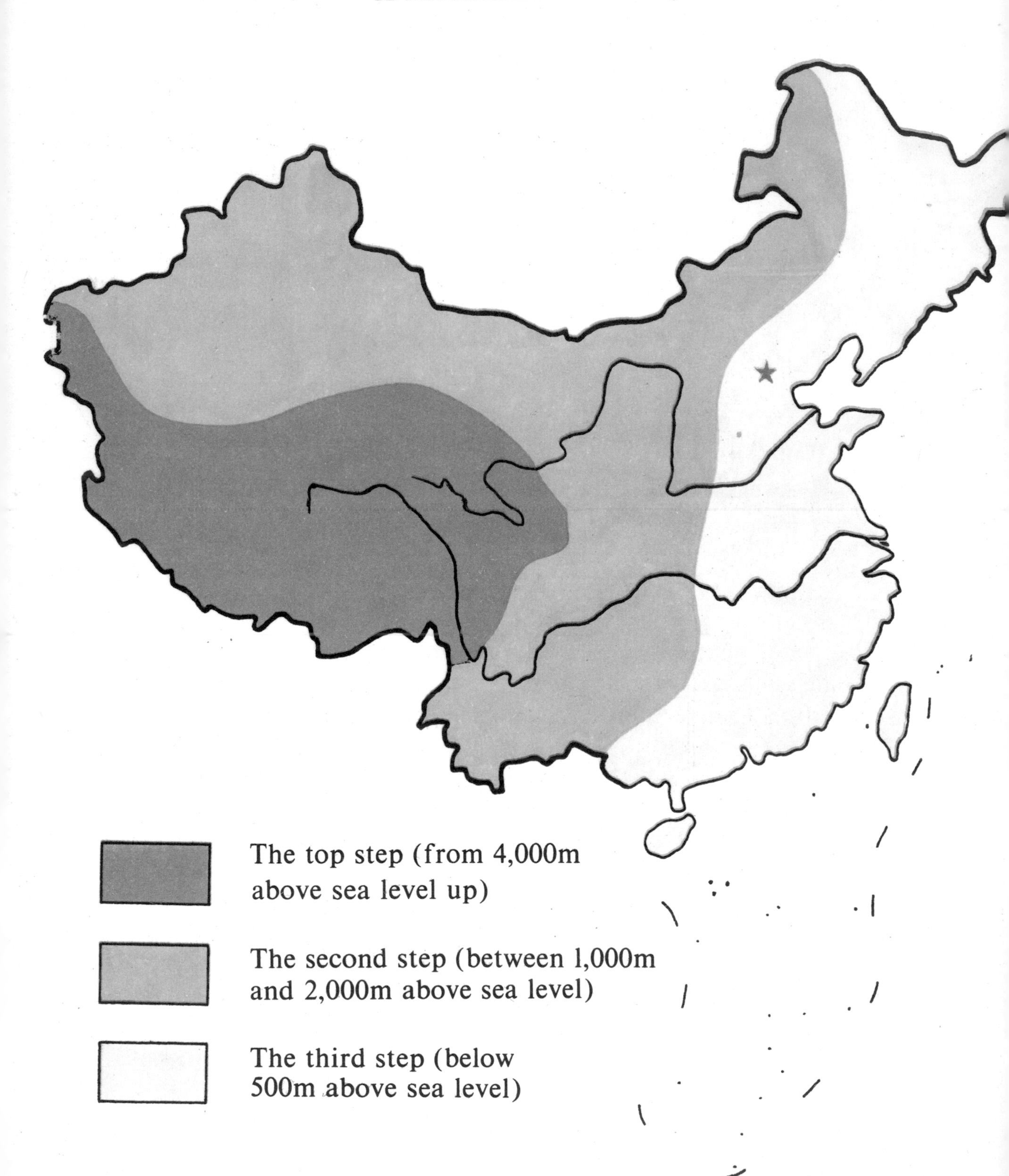

Hills and plateaus cover nearly two thirds of the country's total area. High in the west, low in the east is China's special characteristic in its topography. From a bird's-eye view the land surface of China slopes from west to east in three steps. The top step, the Qinghai-Tibet Plateau in southwestern China, known as "the roof of the world," averages 4,500 metres above sea level. Mount Qomolangma (called Everest by Westerners), the main peak in the Himalayas, is situated on the Sino-Nepalese border. It is 8,848.13 metres above sea level. Qomolangma in the Tibetan language means goddess. Legend says a pretty fairy maiden turned into the mountain. In 1960 and 1975 a dozen Chinese mountaineers climbed Qomolangma's north slope. One of them was Phanthog, a Tibetan woman.

The top step: from 4,000 metres above sea level up.

The second step: between 1,000 and 2,000 metres above sea level.

The third step: below 500 metres above sea level.

A Complex Topography

China has a varied topography—plateaus, hills, mountains, plains and basins. Plains, which are mainly in the central, eastern and northeastern regions, cover one tenth of the country's total area. The plains are China's granaries. In the north and northwest China has vast areas of desert and grassland. The Turpan Depression in Xinjiang is the lowest point in China, reaching 154 metres below sea level. The Sichuan Basin, called land of abundance, is the richest basin in China.

The Yellow River and the Yangtze River

The 6,300-kilometre-long Yangtze River (also called Changjiang, or Long River) is the longest river in China and the third longest river in the world. The middle and lower reaches are alluvial plains, rich and populous areas. The Yellow River is 5,464 kilometres long. It flows from west to east, carrying large quantities of yellow soil from the Loess Plateau, so it is called the Yellow River. The two large rivers start in the mountains in the western part of China and flow to the east to empty into the sea. The Yellow River, in the northern part of China, was the cradle of China's civilization, but it always flooded and brought calamity to the people, so people called it China's disaster river. Over the past thirty years and more much has been done to reinforce dikes and build reservoirs on the upper and middle reaches. Conditions are much better now. The Heilong (Black Dragon) River in the north and the Zhujiang (Pearl River) in the south are other important rivers in China.

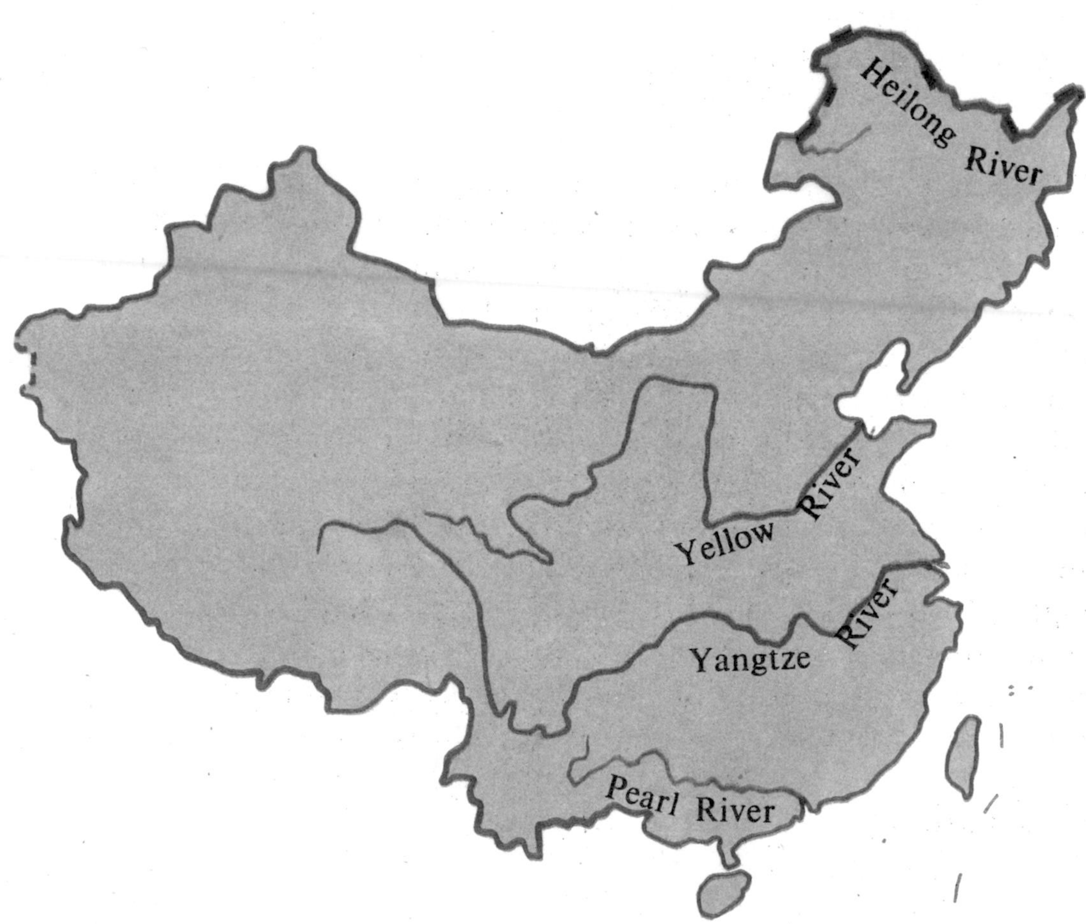
Heilong River
Yellow River
Yangtze River
Pearl River

A Varied Climate

Most of China lies in the warm-temperate zone with four distinct seasons. China's vast area and varied topography create great differences in climate. Hainan Island in the south has summer all year round; northeastern China has severe winter half the year. In the middle of November Harbin, in the north, is covered with snow and ice, while Guangzhou, in the south, is like warm spring. The temperature difference between the two areas is 34°C. China's climate is characterized by monsoonal winds. Coastal areas in the southeast are humid and rainy. Summer brings frequent typhoons and torrential rains. People always take umbrellas with them when they go out. Inland areas in the northwest are very dry and seldom see rain. They experience extremities of temperature in one day. The saying "Fur coats in the morning, gauze at noon; eating watermelon next to the stove" gives a true picture of these parched areas.

Administrative Divisions

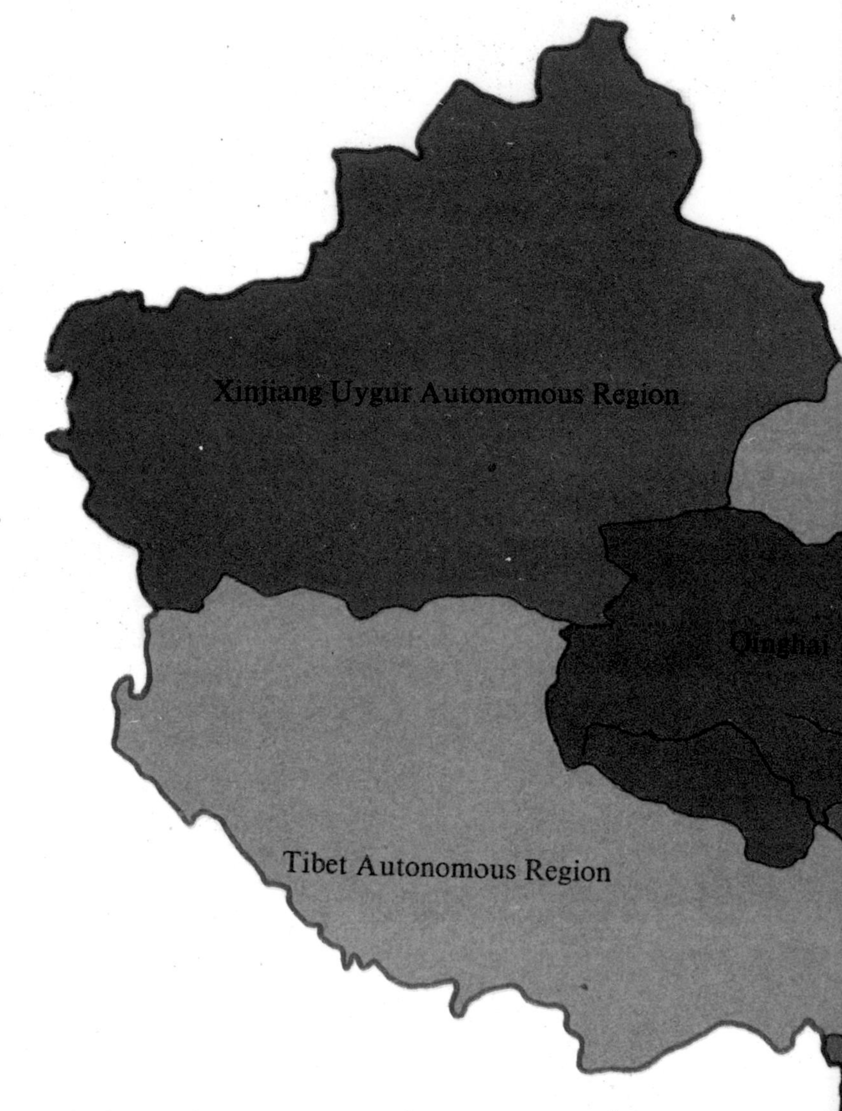

China is divided for administrative purposes into twenty-three provinces, five autonomous regions and three municipalities directly under the central authorities. The five autonomous regions are Inner Mongolia Autonomous Region, Ningxia Hui Autonomous Region, Xinjiang Uygur Autonomous Region, Tibet Autonomous Region and Guangxi Zhuang Autonomous Region. Shanghai, the biggest city in China, has a population of 12 million; Beijing, the second largest, has a population of 9.2 million; Tianjin has a population of 7.7 million. The three municipalities are directly under the central government.

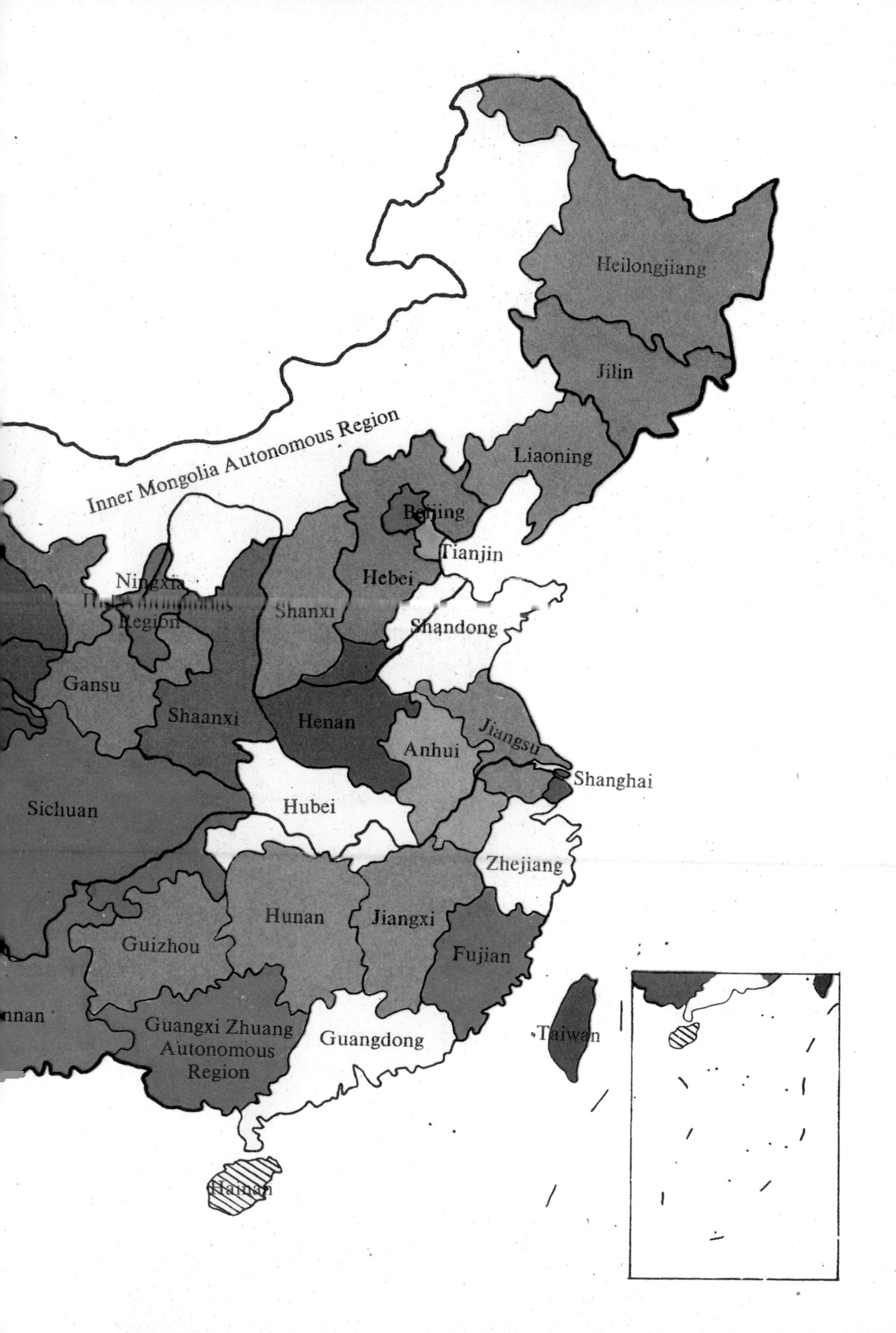
Inner Mongolia Autonomous Region
Heilongjiang
Jilin
Liaoning
Beijing
Tianjin
Hebei
Ningxia
Region
Shanxi
Shandong
Gansu
Shaanxi
Henan
Jiangsu
Anhui
Shanghai
Sichuan
Hubei
Zhejiang
Hunan
Jiangxi
Guizhou
Fujian
Guangxi Zhuang
Autonomous
Region
Guangdong
Taiwan
Hainan

Metasequoia

Metasequoia, a Living Fossil

Forests cover 12.7 percent of China's total area. Of its nearly three thousand kinds of trees the 35-metre-high metasequoia is a living fossil. Metasequoias, grew a hundred million years ago in today's East Asia, North America and Europe, were ruined during the Pleistocene epoch of the Quaternary period. In 1941 over a thousand metasequoias were found in China. Now they have been transplanted in various parts of the world. Besides the metasequoia China has other rare trees, such as the dove tree, ginkgo and Cathay silver fir.

Golden monkey

The Giant Panda

Chinese river dolphin

China has some rare animals, such as the giant panda, golden monkey, white-lipped deer, Chinese river dolphin and Chinese alligator. The giant panda is a national treasure. It is also a living fossil. Everyone loves its comical appearance and mischievous, clumsy movements. Giant pandas live in the mountains in the western part of China. Long ago they were carnivorous animals, but later, because of a change in the environment, they had to live on bamboo. A mature panda

White-lipped deer

Giant panda

Chinese alligator

can eat fifteen kilogrammes of bamboo a day. China is the only country in the world that has wild pandas. Now there are no more than one thousand pandas in the whole world. The panda's favourite kind of food is fountain bamboo. It blossoms every eighty or one hundred years, then large areas of fountain bamboo die. Many pandas die of hunger. In recent years bamboo in the areas where pandas live have blossomed one after the other. The Chinese Government has sent many people up the mountains to look for hungry pandas and bring them down to feeding areas.

Solving the Problem of Feeding the Population

A long time ago China's agriculture was already fairly well developed. After the second century B.C. China began to export silk to countries in Europe. The road the silk traders took was called the Silk Road.

Only 11 percent of China's land is cultivable, resulting in just 0.25 acre of cultivable land per person, much less than the world average of 5.5 acres. China's agriculture was very backward in the old days. In the past thirty years China's population has doubled; the annual output of grain has tripled; the annual output of cotton has increased six times. The Chinese Government has basically solved the problem of feeding the population. At present 80 percent of the population lives in rural areas. Most farm work is still done by manual labour, since there is little agricultural machinery. The main cereal crop is rice, which accounts for half the total output of cereal crops. Other main crops are wheat, corn and sorghum. The main cash crops are cotton, soybeans, peanuts, sugarcane, beetroot, and tobacco.

Developing Industry

China has rich mineral resources. Coal output reached 894 million tons in 1986. Thirty years ago China mainly depended on imported oil. Now the yearly output of crude oil is over 100 million tons, and China has become an oil exporter. China is also rich in iron ore. The output of nonferrous metals, such as antimony, tungsten and aluminium, ranks among the highest in the world. In the past there were few factories. Most industrial products were imported. Now China can produce most such products, including automobiles, aircraft and electronic computers. China has also mastered the complicated technology for manufacturing nuclear missiles. Since China is a developing country, the national income is still comparatively low.

A Multinational Country

China's billion people are divided into fifty-six ethnic groups. The Han nationality makes up 89.5 percent of the total population. Of the minority nationalities the Mongolian, Hui, Tibetan, Uygur, Miao, Yi, Zhuang, Bouyi, Korean and Manchu number over a million people each. The smallest group, the Hezhen, live in the northeast and have only eight hundred people. The fifty-five minority nationalities constitute 10.5 percent of the total population, but they are distributed widely

over the country and occupy 60 percent of the total land area. Most of the minority nationalities inhabit northwestern, southwestern and northeastern border areas. In China every nationality enjoys equal rights. Minority nationalities have the right to use their own spoken and written language. They also enjoy religious freedom. Where they live in compact communities they are given regional autonomy.

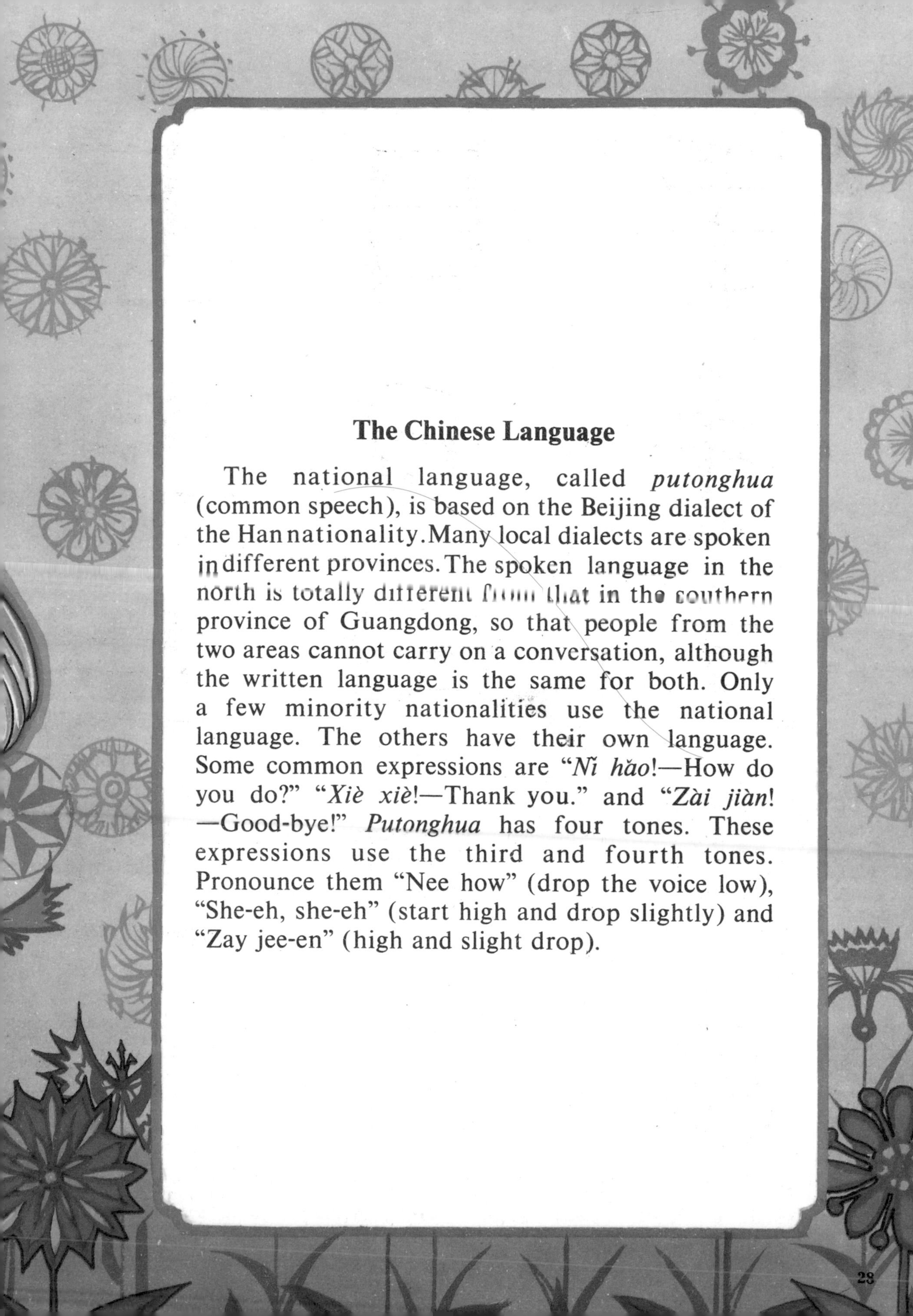

The Chinese Language

The national language, called *putonghua* (common speech), is based on the Beijing dialect of the Han nationality. Many local dialects are spoken in different provinces. The spoken language in the north is totally different from that in the southern province of Guangdong, so that people from the two areas cannot carry on a conversation, although the written language is the same for both. Only a few minority nationalities use the national language. The others have their own language. Some common expressions are "*Nǐ hǎo*!—How do you do?" "*Xiè xiè*!—Thank you." and "*Zài jiàn*! —Good-bye!" *Putonghua* has four tones. These expressions use the third and fourth tones. Pronounce them "Nee how" (drop the voice low), "She-eh, she-eh" (start high and drop slightly) and "Zay jee-en" (high and slight drop).

Learning Chinese

Unlike the written language in many other countries, Chinese characters do not form an alphabetic writing system. Every Chinese character has a meaning, and since there are more than forty thousand characters, it is not easy to remember all of them. Only twenty-five hundred characters are in frequent use. Anyone who masters one thousand characters can read newspapers. Some Chinese characters evolved from pictographs, for instance the character 手 (hand) and 日 (sun). The character 旦 (dawn) puts a horizontal line under 日 (sun), showing the sun rising over the horizon.

Although it is not so difficult to learn Chinese as some people imagine, writing Chinese characters is not so easy as writing words in an alphabetic system. Chinese characters are being simplified to make it easier to learn them. For example, the character 萬 used thirteen strokes before, but now it is written 万, using only three strokes. Also, a Chinese phonetic alphabet, based on the Latin alphabet, has been worked out, providing a supplementary method for learning Chinese that has been greatly welcomed by people studying Chinese.

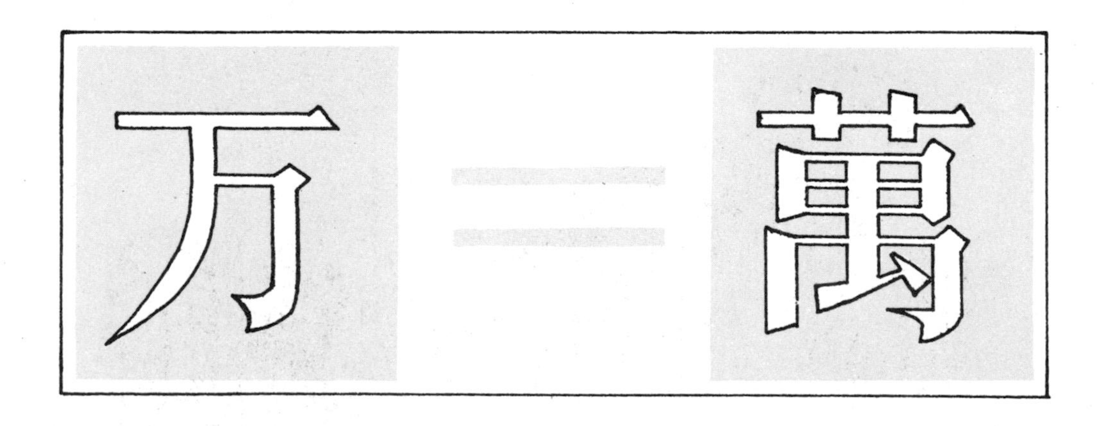

Distinctive Art

In the past the Chinese used a brush to write characters (now people also use a fountain pen and pencil) and calligraphy was a form of art. In ancient times calligraphy and painting were referred to equally. Calligraphy was as important as painting. The traditional Chinese ink-and-wash painting used brush and ink on silk or *xuan* paper (a high-quality paper especially good for traditional Chinese painting). Traditional Chinese painting can be divided into freehand brushwork, characterized by vivid expression and bold outline, and realistic painting, characterized by fine brushwork and close attention to detail. Artists express their emotions and ideas through paintings. China has produced many outstanding painters. The most famous one in modern times was Qi Baishi, who died more than twenty years ago. China also has many ancient coloured murals. The most famous are in the Mogao Grottoes in Dunhuang, Gansu Province. If these murals were lined up, they would stretch as far as twenty kilometres.

Beijing Opera—A Comprehensive Performing Art

Many foreign readers may have seen Beijing opera. *Havoc in Heaven*, a famous Beijing opera, is one of the most popular. Its hero is the Monkey King. Beijing opera was originally performed in the imperial palace in Beijing, so it came to be called Beijing opera. It is a comprehensive performing art, combining recitative, singing, acting, dancing and acrobatics. Besides Beijing opera, China has several hundred plays, including operas and plays introduced from foreign countries.

Confucius (551-479 B.C.)

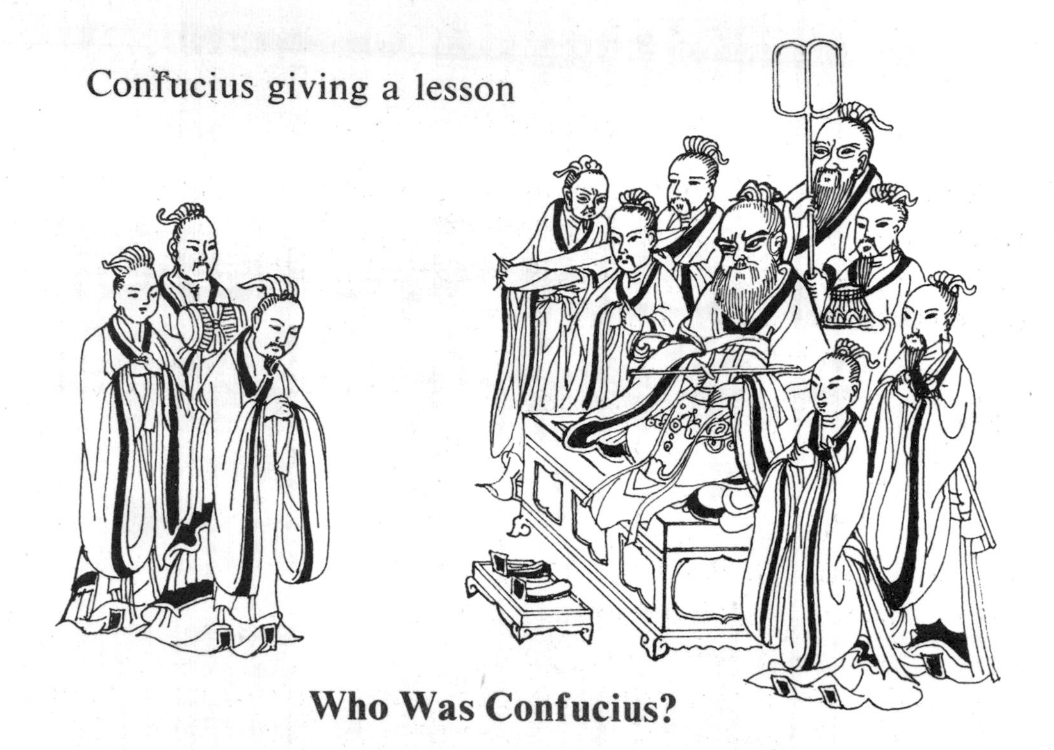
Confucius giving a lesson

Who Was Confucius?

In ancient times there were many scientists, philosophers, writers, statesmen and strategists in China. In foreign countries many people have heard of Confucius. Who was Confucius? He was a great educator during the sixth and fifth centuries B.C. Before Confucius set up a private school for common people, only feudal nobles had the privilege of receiving education. Confucius is said to have had three thousand students. In compiling China's important ancient books he contributed greatly to preserving ancient culture. He was also a thinker. He lived in a transition period from slave society to feudal society. He defended feudal hierarchy, but he opposed the way of might. He advocated a kingly way and travelled to the different states to try to persuade the kings to reform, but no one accepted his suggestions. Though he failed at the time, later generations were greatly influenced by his thinking. Confucius advocated kindness and sympathy towards others, but he held that people were different. Some were èlite and some lowly. Therefore he formulated rules to be observed by different people. For example, officials must be loyal to the king. The king should always show tender affection for the people. The son must obey the father; the father should be kind and gentle to the son. Confucius played an important role in defending the hierarchy of feudal society. For several thousand years Confucius was regarded as a sage in China.

Ancient Poems

Many beautiful poems have been handed down from ancient times. *The Book of Songs*, compiled by Confucius, is a selection of folk songs before the fourth century B.C. Here is a poem that depicts the resentment of peasants towards rulers.

O monster rats! O monster rats!
Eat not our millet, we implore.
Three years we've borne with you,
And still our presence you ignore.
Now we abandon you
And to yon pleasant lands repair.
O pleasant lands! O pleasant lands!
A refuge have we surely there.

Li Bai, who lived twelve hundred years ago, is one of China's most famous poets. Here is one of his poems.

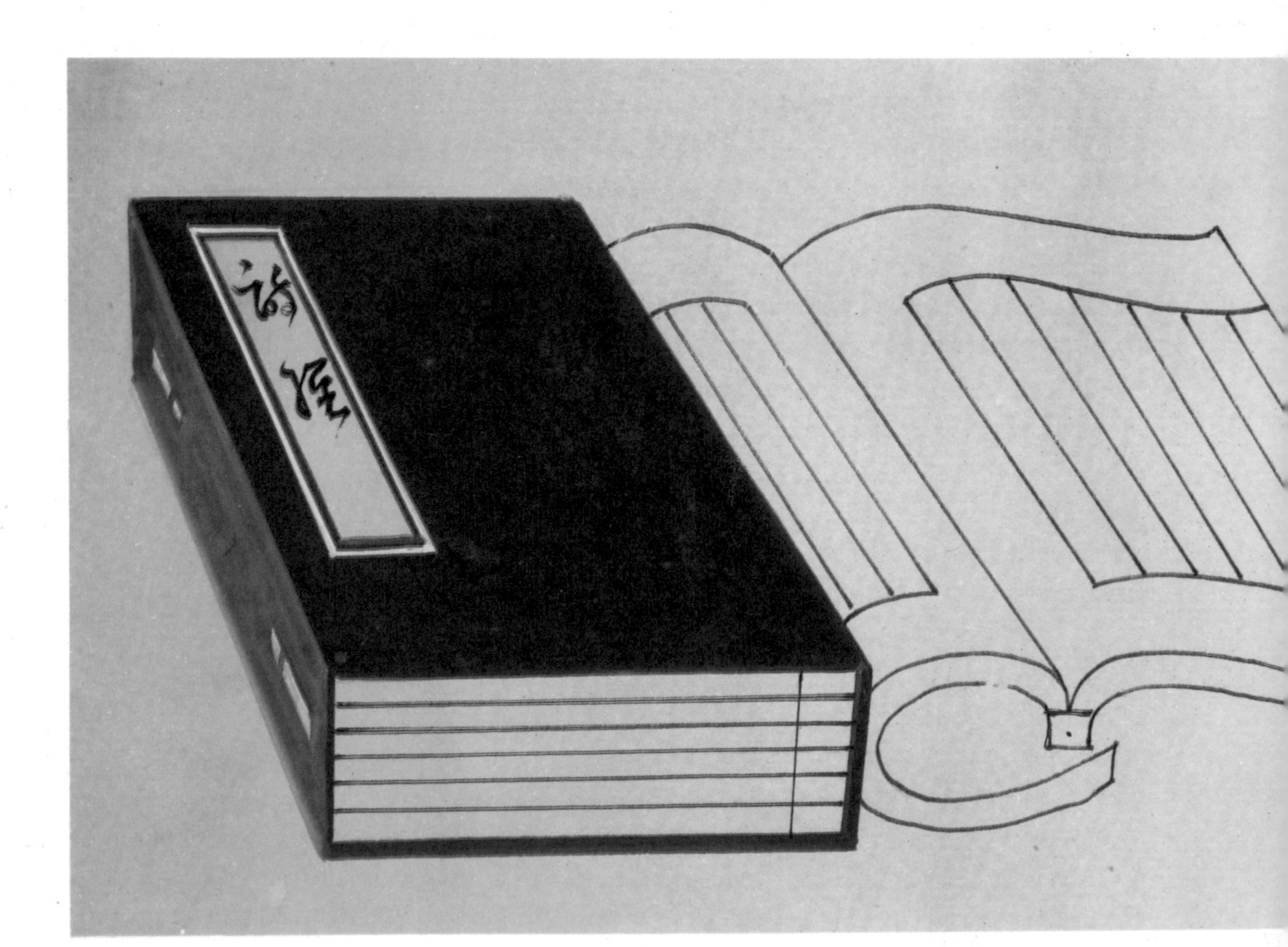

Li Bai (701-762)

So bright a gleam on the foot of my bed—
Could there have been a frost already?
Lifting myself to look, I found that it was moonlight.
Sinking back again, I thought suddenly of home.

The Great Wall

Men in space have said that only two manmade projects —land reclaimed from the sea in the Netherlands and the Great Wall in China—could be seen on earth. Usually people think that the Great Wall was built during the Qin Dynasty, but actually its beginnings can be traced back as far as the seventh century B.C. At that time rival feudal kingdoms built walls around their territories for self-protection. Following unification of the separate kingdoms under Qin Shi Huang (first emperor of the Qin) in the third century B.C. the existing fortifications were linked up, constructing an important barrier against invasion by nomadic tribes to the north. The total length was about 5,000 kilometres. Most sections of the Qin Dynasty wall have been damaged. The present wall was built during the fourteenth century; its total length was 6,300 kilometres, and it stretched from the sea in the east to the northwestern part of China, crossing mountains, the Yellow River and desert. It takes only a little more than an hour to visit the Great Wall from Beijing.

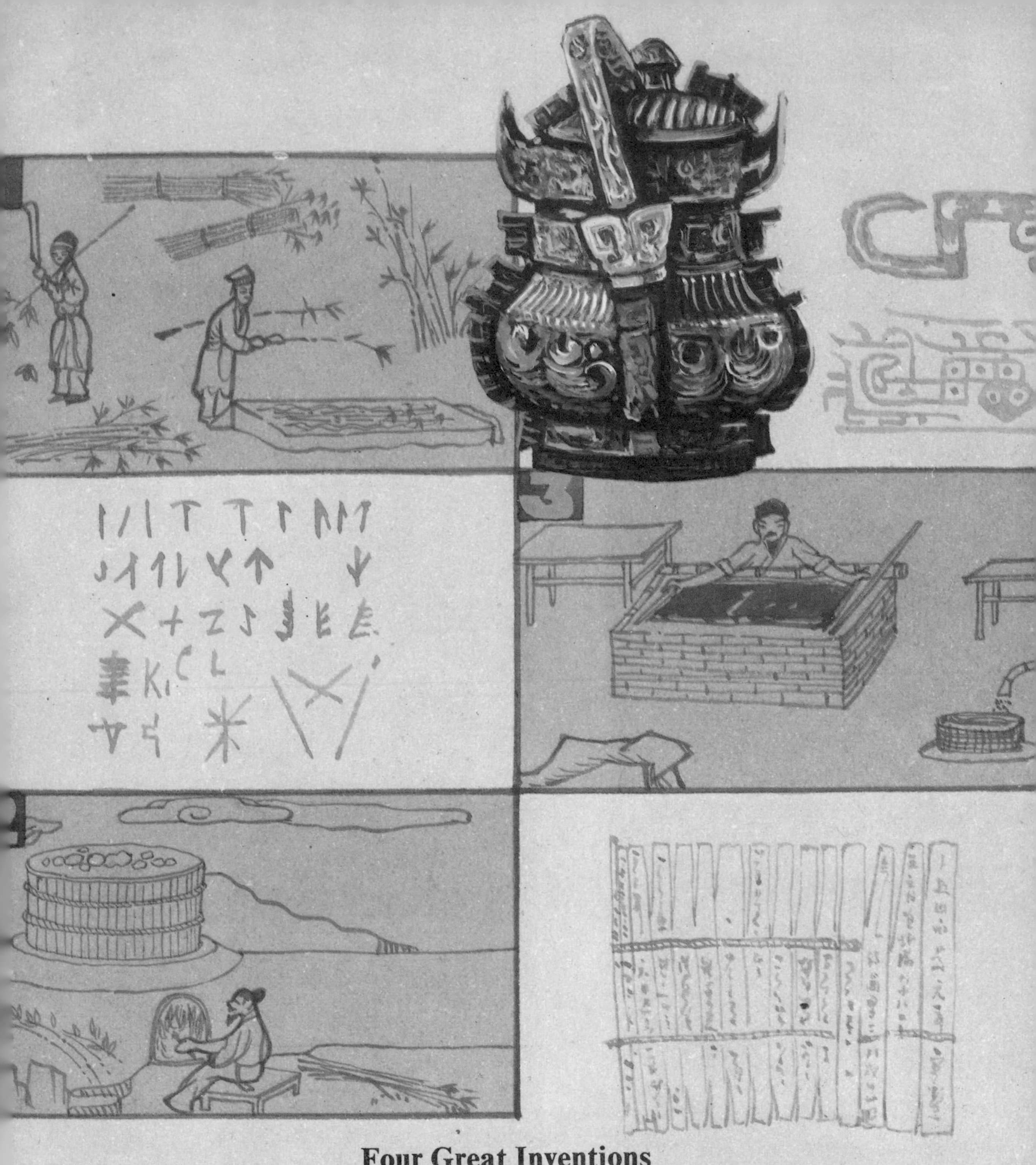

Four Great Inventions

Of the many important inventions in ancient China paper making, printing, the compass and gunpowder are the most famous. At first characters were inscribed on tortoise shell and ox bones; afterwards, they were inscribed on bronze, stone,

bamboo slips or silk fabric. It was most inconvenient. It is said that Qin Shi Huang read documents written on flat strips of bamboo that weighed more than fifty kilogrammes. At the beginning of the second century China began to produce

writing paper made from bark fibre and hemp. Paper making furthered the spread of culture and science.

In the sixth century China invented block printing, whereby characters were carved into wooden blocks, then printed on

paper. Movable type was invented in the eleventh century and introduced to Europe in the thirteenth century.

In the first century B.C. a primitive compass called *sinan*

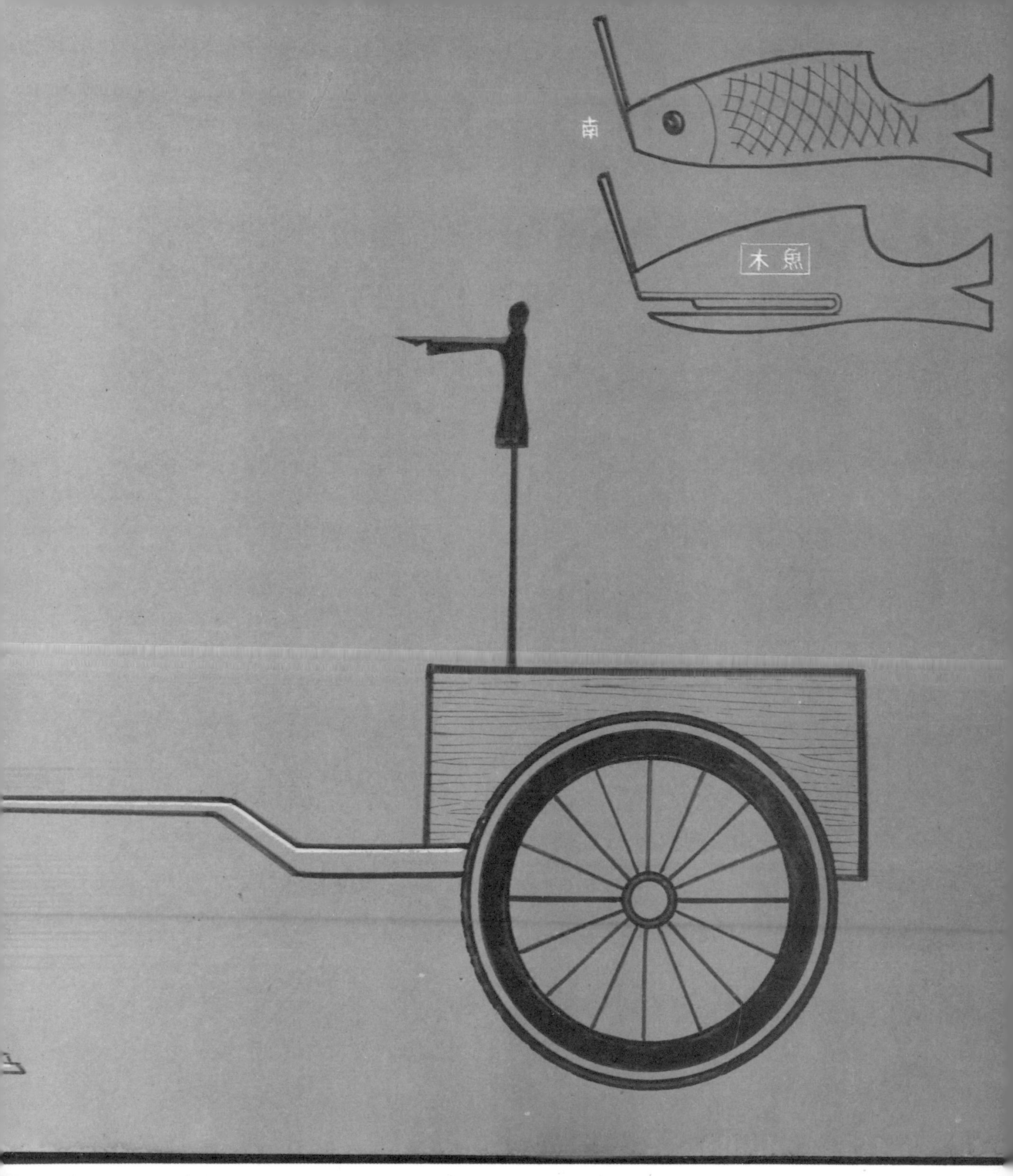

(controlling the south) was invented in China when people discovered magnetic attraction. In the eleventh century China began to use the compass in navigation as Chinese vessels sailed

to Southeast Asia and the western shores of Africa.

Gunpowder was also invented very early in China. In the tenth century China began to use gunpowder in battles. The

gunpowder was tied to arrowheads and shot. Later on the rifle and cannon were invented. In the thirteenth century Arab countries spread firearms to European countries.

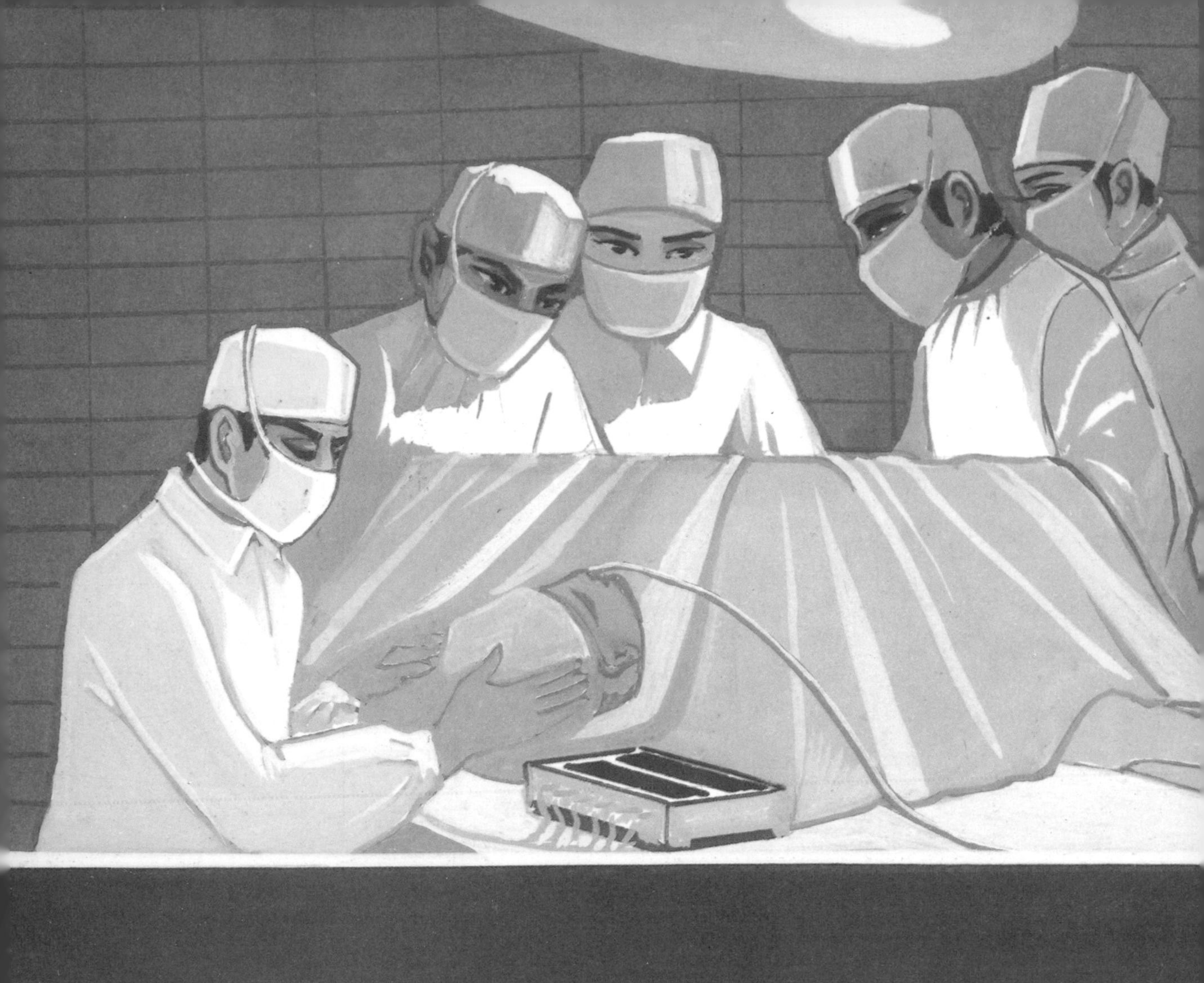

Traditional Chinese Medicine

In recent years China's acupuncture and moxibustion have become popular in foreign countries because they are simple to apply, safe, economical and quick acting. They are effective for more than three hundred diseases, especially for coma caused by head injury, germ-caused illness, hemiplegia and rheumatism. Acupuncture anaesthesia has been used successfully in surgical operations.

China's traditional medicine long ago spread to Asian countries such as Japan and Korea. To diagnose diseases from their symptoms doctors of traditional medicine use four methods: inquiring as to the patient's condition, observing the patient's colour, listening to the patient's breathing and feeling

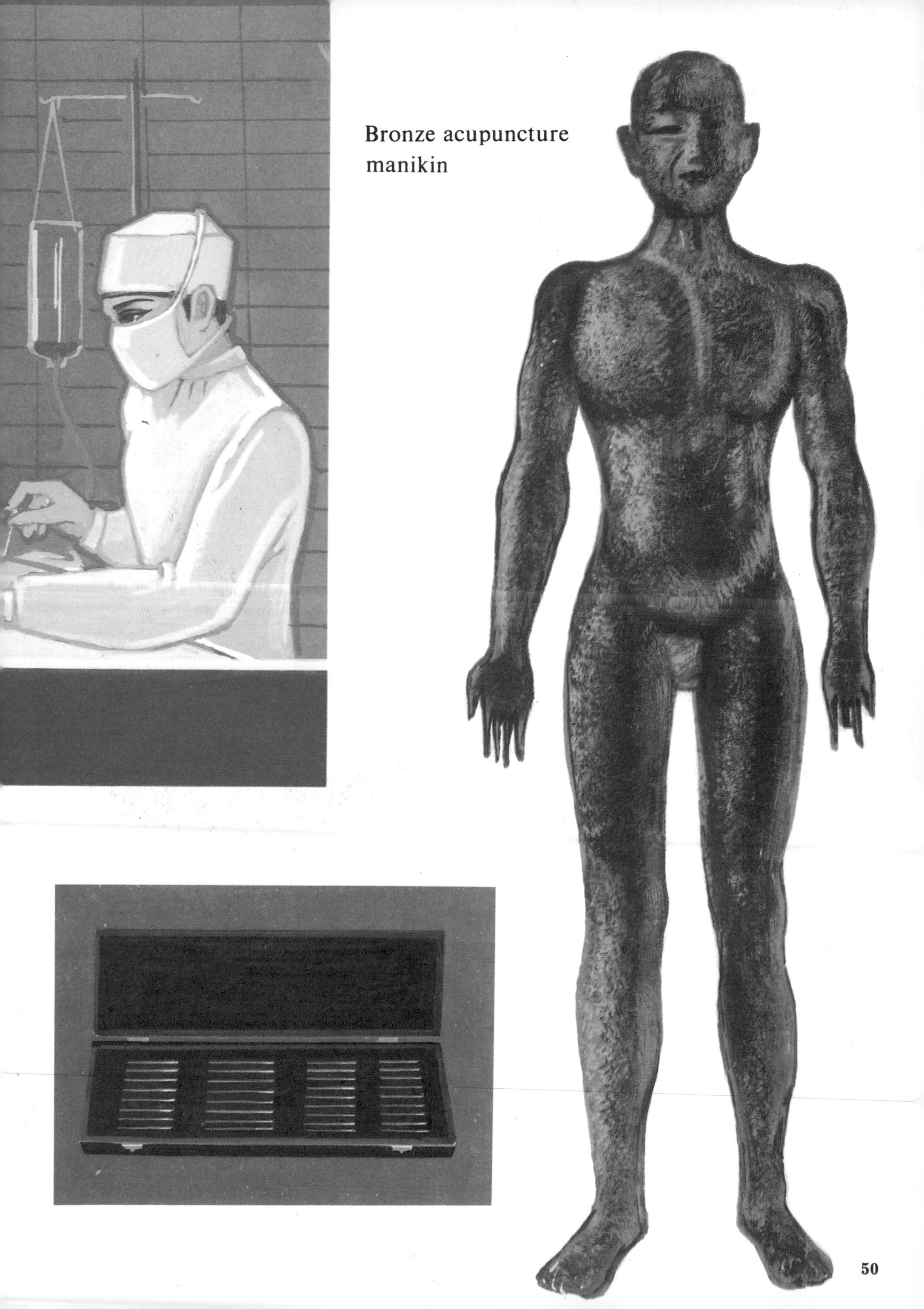

Bronze acupuncture manikin

the patient's pulse. Traditional Chinese medicine has good methods to cure certain diseases. For example, cholelithiasis can be cured by taking Chinese medicine and does not require a surgical operation. Currently traditional Chinese medicine and Western medicine are being combined in medical work.

Chinese Cuisine

Many cities in the world have Chinese restaurants, and Chinese food is greatly liked. Chinese cuisine forms a component part of China's ancient culture. China has eight schools of culinary art, each with its special characteristics. The most famous are Guangdong, Sichuan, Jiangsu and Shandong. Jiangsu dishes are light and sweet and have great variety. There are more than a hundred ways to prepare freshwater fish. Sichuan dishes are spicy hot. Guangdong dishes are half cooked. Shandong dishes are rather salty and most are quick-fried.

Southerners eat mainly rice, while northerners eat mainly food made of flour, such as steamed bread and noodles.

The Sun Yat-sen Mausoleum

Dr. Sun Yat-sen (1866-1925)

Decline of Feudal China

China's ancient civilization dates back four thousand years, yet in the nineteenth century China became a backward country. What was the reason?

In 1840 Britain launched the Opium War because China prohibited its opium trade. The corrupt Qing government could not withstand the enemy's blows. From then on, China turned step by step into a country dominated by foreign powers, forced repeatedly to sign unequal treaties, cede territory and pay indemnities. China grew weaker and weaker. The Chinese people struggled against the despotic rule of the Qing government, until finally the Revolution of 1911, led by Dr. Sun Yat-sen, put an end to the two-thousand-year-old feudal monarchy and the Republic of China was founded. Dr. Sun Yat-sen was a great forerunner of China's democratic revolution. People will always remember him.

The Founding of New China

Though the Revolution of 1911 overthrew the Qing Dynasty, antidemocratic forces were very powerful. Colluding with the imperialists, warlords waged continual wars. The reactionary forces arrested China's progress. Dr. Sun Yat-sen's plan failed. The gains of the Revolution of 1911 were lost. In fact, China was divided up into spheres of influence among the imperialist powers. Japan, France, Britain and other countries invaded China and established concessions. Many foreign countries still had concessions in China in 1945 when the anti-Japanese War ended. China regained the large territory occupied by Japan after Japan was defeated, but the Kuomintang government was very corrupt and China was still poor and backward. People did not have any democratic rights. The Chinese Communist Party, under the leadership of Mao Zedong, Zhou Enlai and Zhu De,

led the Chinese people in a hard struggle for many years. Finally the Chinese people overthrew the rule of the Kuomintang, and the People's Republic of China was founded on October 1, 1949. The founding ceremony was held in Beijing and Chairman Mao Zedong himself raised the first national flag—a red flag with five yellow stars. October 1 was declared China's National Day.

What do the five yellow stars represent? The big star stands for the party in power—the Communist Party of China. The four small stars stand for the people of all nationalities rallying around the Party.

The founding of the People's Republic of China marked the victory of the Chinese revolution. China shook off the yoke of feudalism and colonialism and attained true independence.

The Chinese people's aim was to form an ideal society free from exploitation of man by man—a socialist country with a highly developed economy and culture.

Beijing—An Ancient and A New City

Beijing, the capital of New China, is also one of China's ancient capitals. A thousand years ago the Qidan (Khitan), who

established the Liao Dynasty, were the first to make Beijing their capital. Afterwards many dynasties made Beijing their

capital. The former imperial palace of the Ming and Qing dynasties is still preserved intact. Former imperial garderns and many ancient buildings have also been preserved.

Tiananmen (Gate of Heavenly Peace) stands in front of the entrance to the imperial palace. Tiananmen Square, directly south of Tiananmen, is the centre of Beijing and can hold five hundred thousand people for a mass rally. On the west side of the square is the Great Hall of the People, where the National People's Congress convenes. It is the centre of the country's political activity. Hundreds of thousands of people helped in constructing it, taking only ten months to build it in 1958.